W9-BBX-390

Sunburns, Twisters, and Thunderclaps

By Janice Parker

RSVP®

RAINTREE
STECK-VAUGHN
P U B L I S H E R S
A Steck-Vaughn Company

Austin, Texas

www.steck-vaughn.com

Published by Raintree Steck-Vaughn, an imprint of Steck-Vaughn Company

Library of Congress Cataloging-in-Publication Data

Parker, Janice.
  Sunburns, twisters, and thunderclaps /
 by Janice Parker.
   p. cm. — (Science [at] work)
 In ser. statement "[at]" appears as the at symbol.
 Includes bibliographical references and index.
 Summary: Discusses how sun, wind, and water make up the different kinds of weather and how we examine, measure, and predict weather.
 ISBN 0-7398-0131-7
 1. Meteorology—Juvenile literature. [1. Weather. 2. Meteorology.]
I. Title. II. Series: Science [at] work (Austin, Tex.)
QC863.5.P36 1999
551.5—DC21   98-50030
                  CIP
                  AC

Printed and bound in Canada
1 2 3 4 5 6 7 8 9 0 03 02 01 00 99

Project Coordinator
Ann Sullivan
Content Validator
Lois Edwards
Design and Illustration
Warren Clark
Copy Editors
Elizabeth Entrup
Leslie Strudwick
Layout
Chantelle Sales

Photograph Credits
Every reasonable effort has been made to trace ownership and to obtain permission to reprint copyright material. The publishers would be pleased to have any errors or omissions brought to their attention so that they may be corrected in subsequent printings.

Atmospherics Incorporated: page 34; **Dave Butler**: pages 11 top, 13 bottom; **Corel Corporation**: cover top left, pages 4 middle, 6 left, 10 top, 11 bottom, 16, 18 left, 19 top, 21 bottom, 23 bottom, 27, 28 top, 30 top, right, 32 bottom, 42, 43 left, 44; **Gary Neil Corbett**: pages 6 top, 10 bottom, 23 top, 30 left, 31 top; **DigitalVision**: page 39 middle; **John Fowler**: page 29; **GM Media**: page 9; **Paul Hickson**: page 14; **V.C. Last**: pages 12, 20 top, 33; **Tom Myers**: pages 18 top, 20 bottom, 21 top, 28 left, 31 bottom, 32 top, 35, 40, 41, 43 right; **National Aeronautics and Space Administration**: pages 7, 15; **National Oceanic and Atmospheric Administration**: page 17; **Tom Stack and Associates**: cover top right, pages 13 top, 25 top (Scott Norquay), cover background, 4 bottom, 36 (Wm. L. Wantland), 4 top (Merrilee Thomas), 25 bottom (Brian Parker), 38 (Therisa Stack), 39 bottom (TSADO/NCDC/NOAA).

Contents

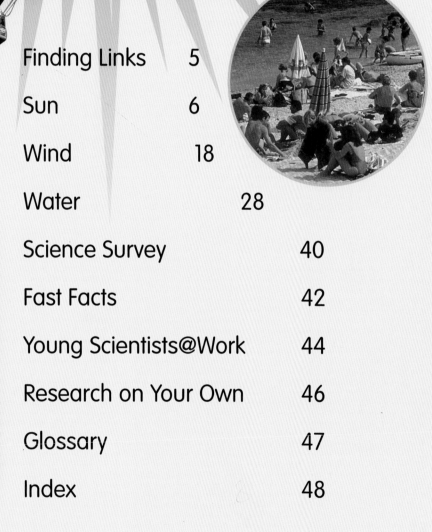

Have you ever seen a twister,

had a sunburn,

or watched your dog hide from a thunderclap?

If so, you have experienced just three of the thousands of effects the weather can have on your life. Weather is caused by the conditions that exist in the air around you. It can be hot, cold, wet, or dry. It can be windy, calm, stormy, or humid.

All weather has four main ingredients: temperature, wind, water, and air pressure. We know a great deal about the science at work in making weather, but not enough to make weather predictable. Weather can change without warning. It can sometimes work silently, such as when the Sun burns your skin. Or it can make a grand entrance, as tornadoes and hurricanes do, leaving nothing standing in its path.

FINDING LINKS

Society

The community you live in is affected by weather conditions. Businesses such as the airline industry depend upon good weather for the safety of their passengers and crew. Farmers depend on good weather to grow their crops. Other people then depend on good crops for food.

The Environment

Sometimes people affect the weather, but in a negative way. Changes to Earth's environment due to pollution can cause weather conditions like smog and **acid rain**.

Technology

Because of weather's impact on their lives, people have always tried to learn about and control the weather. Many different kinds of technology are connected with weather—everything from weather vanes to satellites. People have even found technology to harness Sun and wind energy for human use.

Careers

You may want to learn more about weather by entering a weather-related career such as meteorology. Even if you do not want to study the weather full-time, learning more about the weather can help you every day.

Sun

"The weather
will be sunny
and warm
today."

The Sun is the key to life on Earth.
Without the Sun, the planet would freeze,
and all animals that rely on its energy for
plant growth and food would die. People who
lived in ancient times worshiped the Sun. They
knew of its great importance in maintaining
life on Earth. However, they did not understand
the science behind the Sun's power. For example,
we now understand some of the ways the Sun's
energy influences weather. Everything from wind
and temperature to tornadoes and hurricanes is
affected by the Sun.

What is the Sun?

The Sun is a giant ball of fiery gases 93 million miles (150 million km) from Earth. It is our closest star and one of the hundred billion stars in our galaxy.

The Sun sends out large amounts of energy in all directions. Only a tiny amount of that energy reaches Earth, about two-billionths of the total output. But it is enough energy to provide plenty of light and heat for all the plants and animals on Earth. Without the Sun's energy, the temperature on Earth would be no higher than −418°F (−250°C).

The Sun's energy arrives on Earth as different types of radiant energy, or rays. Light is simply the kind of ray that you can see. Although you cannot see **infrared** rays, you can feel them. When infrared rays hit your skin, or any other object, the energy usually turns into heat. Nearly all of the heat on Earth comes from the infrared rays of sunshine.

Fiery surface

The temperature on the surface of the Sun is 10,832°F (6,000°C). The Sun's core reaches a temperature of about 27,000,000°F (15,000,000°C).

BYTE-SIZED FACT

The Sun has harmful rays that can cause sunburns and skin cancer. Most of these rays are trapped high up in the **atmosphere** by a special form of oxygen called ozone. Ozone forms a protective layer surrounding Earth that is about 22 miles (35 km) above the ground.

What makes the seasons?

Seasons are caused when different amounts of the Sun's energy reach Earth at different times of the year. Earth's **axis** is tilted as it makes its yearlong **orbit** around the Sun. When it is summer in the Northern **Hemisphere**, the Sun's rays strike the top half of Earth directly. At the same time, the rays reaching the Southern Hemisphere are more indirect. They cover a much larger area, so the region is cooler. During the spring and autumn, the Sun is most direct at the **equator**.

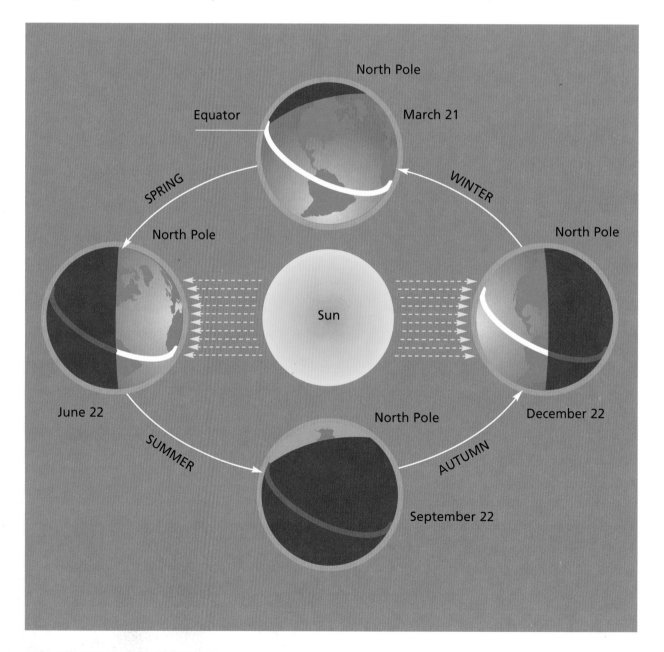

Solar Energy

Energy from the Sun warms Earth's atmosphere, making winds blow and ocean currents flow.

The Sun's energy is part of the "fuel" for plants to grow. Fuels such as gasoline are solar energy stored much earlier in Earth's history. Oil and gas are formed from the decayed bodies of plants and animals that received energy from the Sun, either directly or indirectly.

Solar technology uses the Sun's power to produce energy for human societies. Some ancient aboriginal groups built their homes so that they could get as much light and warmth

Sunraycer, a solar car, won the World Solar Challenge race. Solar power may be an important source of energy in the future. It causes little pollution and is almost always available.

from the Sun as possible. Some of these homes were made from clay, which absorbed the Sun's heat and kept the homes warm in the winter.

Today scientists use solar energy in many ways. **Solar** **panels** make electricity from the Sun's rays. This electricity is then stored in a battery where it can be used later. The batteries can be used to run televisions, stereos, lights, and computers.

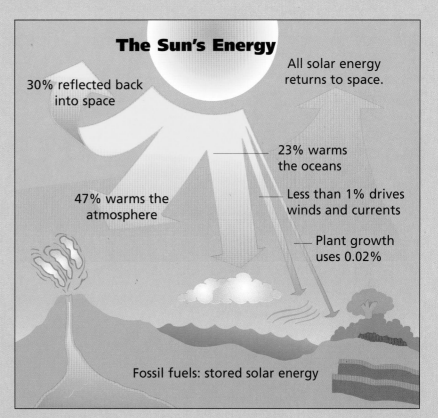

The Sun's Energy

30% reflected back into space

All solar energy returns to space.

47% warms the atmosphere

23% warms the oceans

Less than 1% drives winds and currents

Plant growth uses 0.02%

Fossil fuels: stored solar energy

Where does the Sun's energy go?

When the Sun's rays reach Earth, the energy may be absorbed by land, water, or air. In each case the results are quite different.

Air absorbs some of the Sun's energy as the rays pass through. But most of the rays move through the air until they reach water or land.

City buildings trap more heat than country land, so cities tend to be warmer than surrounding regions.

Land features such as soil, rocks, and pavement become warm when they absorb the Sun's energy. As the temperature of the land rises, some of the heat is given off into the air close to the ground. This makes the air temperature rise. Then, when the air moves, it carries the heat from one place to another.

When water absorbs sun rays, the energy causes some of the water to **evaporate** and enter the air as water vapor. This creates **humidity** and clouds.

BYTE-SIZED FACT

Water can absorb a lot of heat without showing much of an increase in temperature. Land that is near oceans and large lakes does not become as warm as land that is far from bodies of water. However, water also holds onto its heat energy longer than land does. For this reason, coastal cities stay warmer in the winter than inland cities.

How do we measure temperature?

Temperature is measured by thermometers. Scientists in the 17th century realized that water always boils and freezes at the same temperatures. This discovery helped scientists make a temperature scale. The scale allowed all scientists to measure temperature with the same numbers.

Thermometers can use both Celsius and Fahrenheit scales.

The hottest temperatures on Earth have been recorded in desert areas.

The German scientist Gabriel Fahrenheit was the first to use **mercury** in thermometers. Mercury responds quickly to temperature changes, swelling when it gets warmer and shrinking when it gets colder. Fahrenheit made a temperature scale that is still used today. He set 0°F as the lowest winter temperature where he lived in Germany. Water freezes at 32°F and boils at 212°F.

In 1742 Anders Celsius, a Swedish astronomer, developed a scale with simpler numbers. He made the freezing point of water 0°C and the boiling point 100°C. His system is widely used today, especially by scientists, who find the system easier to use than the Fahrenheit method.

> **BYTE-SIZED FACT**
>
> Vostok, Antarctica, is the coldest place on Earth, where the temperature has dropped to −126.9°F (−88.3°C). The hottest place on Earth is Al'Aziziyah, Libya, where it has been as hot as 136.4°F (58°C).

How did people forecast weather in the past?

For centuries, people have tried to learn about and forecast the weather. Hundreds of years ago, people in Europe believed that animal behavior changed depending on the weather. For example, people believed that hedgehogs could predict the end of winter. When European settlers arrived in North America, they could not find any hedgehogs, so they decided to use groundhogs instead.

According to tradition, groundhogs end their hibernation on February 2nd, signaling the end of winter. If a groundhog comes out of the ground and sees its shadow, says the tradition, it gets frightened and runs back into the ground. This means there will be 6 more weeks of winter. Scientists who have studied the groundhog theory have concluded that this traditional method of forecasting weather does not work.

A tradition that has a history of more success is the *Old Farmers' Almanac*. First published in 1792, the *Old Farmers' Almanac* gives information about weather, the rise and set of the Sun, and the tides. Its weather forecasts are correct about 80 percent of the time— a very good rate. The forecasts are given on the basis of weather folklore and a secret scientific formula. Many farmers and other people whose jobs depend on the weather rely on the advice in the *Old Farmers' Almanac*.

People who live where there are cold winters are eager to find out if the groundhog will see its shadow.

BYTE-SIZED FACT

The *Old Farmers' Almanac* is so accurate that the United States government almost prevented it from being published during World War II. In 1942 a German spy was caught by officials on Long Island, New York. The spy had a copy of the *Old Farmers' Almanac* in his pocket. The government was worried that the publication could supply the enemy with important information. In the end it was decided that the almanac could continue to be published.

Meteorologist

Today the weather is forecast by meteorologists.

Meteorologists use technology such as computers, satellites, and radar to help them forecast the weather. They tell people what the day-to-day weather is and what can be expected for the next few months. They also warn people about dangerous weather systems, such as tornadoes and hurricanes.

Meteorologists research ways to prevent weather that is dangerous to humans. Most meteorologists work in government positions and have a degree in **meteorology**.

Technology helps meteorologists make accurate weather forecasts.

BYTE-SIZED FACT

Even with advanced technology, many meteorologists believe accurate daily weather forecasts beyond 2 weeks are impossible.

Did humans cause the greenhouse effect?

The "greenhouse effect" is the popular term for how the atmosphere helps warm the global **ecosystem**. Just as glass on a greenhouse holds the Sun's warmth inside, so the atmosphere traps heat near Earth's surface and keeps Earth warm. The greenhouse effect makes Earth a good planet for living things.

As a natural part of Earth's greenhouse effect, the planet periodically warms and cools. Some people are concerned about the present warming trend because it is happening faster than ever before. Many human activities are adding greenhouse gases like carbon dioxide and methane to the atmosphere. Activities that produce these gases include farming, coal mining, and flying airplanes.

We cannot be sure how global warming will affect us in the future. If greenhouse gases in the atmosphere increase, global temperatures might rise to a level that could become very dangerous. If Earth's water warms and expands, polar ice and glaciers may melt. Some coastal areas may be permanently flooded, and people would lose their homes. Changing temperatures could also mean crops will not grow well, causing food shortages in some areas.

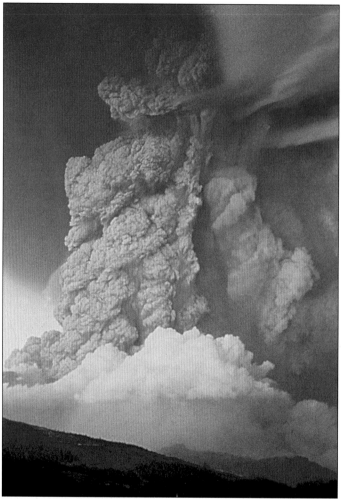

Volcanic eruptions send many chemical particles into the air. These particles screen out sunlight, making global warming more difficult to measure.

BYTE-SIZED FACT The average car gives off more than its own weight in carbon dioxide each year. Driving fast burns more fuel and causes more pollution than driving slowly for the same distance.

The Ozone Hole

In the 1970s, scientists studying the atmosphere in Antarctica began to suspect that the ozone layer was thinning.

This was confirmed in 1985. Chemicals called **chlorofluorocarbons (CFCs)** have damaged the ozone that protects Earth. CFCs are made by people and used in some spray cans, insulation, cleaning materials, refrigerators, and air conditioning. Using something made with CFCs releases the chemical into the air.

The ozone has become thinnest at the South Pole. The cold climate has the right conditions for chemicals in the air to destroy ozone. In 1995 the "hole" in the ozone was as big as Europe. Some ozone loss also happens over the North Pole.

As the ozone layer thins, and more ultraviolet rays reach Earth, the health of animals and plants is endangered, both on land and in the ocean. Ozone loss may also affect the climate.

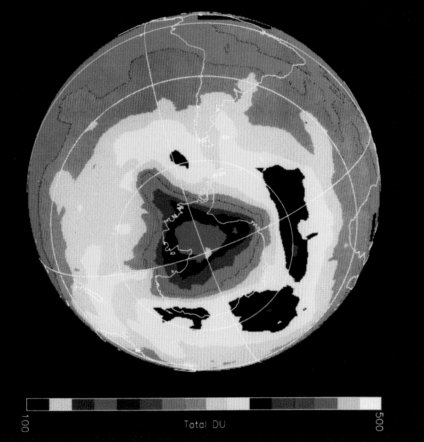

100   Total DU   500

Ozone loss over 10 years
The ozone layer is thinnest at the poles during early spring, but the layer partially recovers in the summer and the fall.

Ozone can be replaced, although it will take at least another 70 years for the layer to recover from the damage that has been done so far. CFCs can last from 60 million to 400 million years. Many countries have stopped making CFCs, but some replacement chemicals also damage the ozone layer.

How can the Sun's rays be deadly?

Some of the Sun's energy is necessary for life, but too much can be harmful. Ultraviolet (UV) rays from the Sun can cause skin cancer, including the deadly form known as melanoma. Other effects of UV rays include damaged eyesight and, possibly, weaker defenses against infection. The United States government has estimated that every one percent of ozone loss causes thousands more cases of skin cancer each year, and blindness in 100,000 people worldwide. Ultraviolet radiation also harms water animals such as plankton, shellfish, and fish. Too much UV sunlight has caused sheep to go blind in southern Chile. Some frog species could be at risk of extinction because UV rays damage their eggs. Crops grow smaller leaves if UV rays increase, harming food production.

Sunscreens are chemical creams that help to block UV rays and prevent damage to the skin.

BYTE-SIZED FACT

Did you know that a sunburn will not turn into a suntan? Sunburns and suntans are caused by different types of UV rays. A sunburn may become lighter as it heals, but it will never become a suntan.

Ultraviolet Radiation

Since the early 1990s, scientists, educators, and news media have reported on the dangers of ultraviolet radiation.

A measuring scale, called the UV index, has been developed to describe the strength of UV radiation. In many sunny climates, a daily UV index is given with the weather to warn people about the danger from the Sun's rays. Even some cooler climates now issue a UV warning during summer months.

When skin is exposed to UV light, it produces **melanin**, which causes the skin to darken. A suntan is your body's way of protecting itself from damaging UV light. Darker skin, while it can still become sunburned, is less likely to suffer damage than lighter skin. Darker skin has more melanin, so it filters out more UV light naturally.

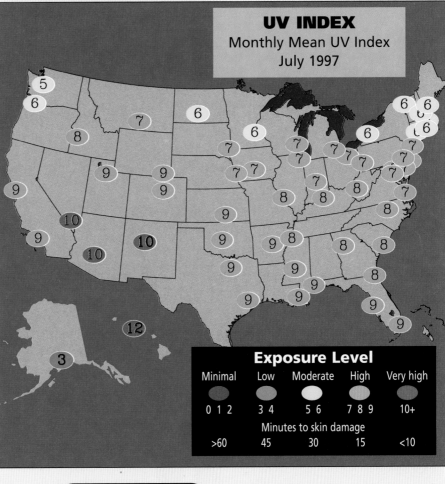

UV INDEX
Monthly Mean UV Index
July 1997

Exposure Level

Minimal	Low	Moderate	High	Very high
0 1 2	3 4	5 6	7 8 9	10+

Minutes to skin damage

| >60 | 45 | 30 | 15 | <10 |

Here is your challenge:

Look at the UV index and the map. What areas would have the lowest level of UV rays? The highest? In what place would it be most dangerous to be out in the Sun?

Wind

"Wind is out of the southwest with gusts of up to 30 miles per hour."

Wind is the movement of air. Earth is surrounded by a blanket of air called the atmosphere. The atmosphere is about 186 miles (300 km) thick. This may seem very thick, but compared to Earth's size, the atmosphere is like the skin on an apple. The atmosphere gets thinner on its outer edges. This means there are fewer particles of air higher up in the atmosphere than there are close to Earth's surface. Air movement, and therefore wind, begins with heat from the Sun.

What makes the wind blow?

The wind blows for the same reason that hot-air balloons rise. Air moves, and heat goes up.

Ground that is warmed by the Sun transfers heat to the air. Air **molecules** move faster when they are heated, bumping into each other more and more forcefully. The energetic molecules push one another apart, and the air becomes thinner and lighter. Air will always move from areas where there are many air molecules to areas where there are few. The light air rises like a bubble. At the same time, heavier, cooler air moves in below to take its place. This causes the air to circulate. The basic rule is that whenever warm air and cool air meet, the wind will blow.

Coastal areas have winds created by differences in temperature between the land and the ocean. Land cools more quickly than water, but it also heats faster.

BYTE-SIZED FACT
Air blowing away from land is called a land breeze. Air blowing in from the ocean is called a sea breeze.

DAY
Warm air rises from the land.
Cool air moves in to take its place.

NIGHT
Cool air moves in to take its place.
Warm air rises from the ocean.

How do we measure the wind?

Wind vanes, also called weather vanes, are used to tell wind direction. As wind hits the side of a weather vane, the vane is pushed around so that it points into the wind.

Airports often use wind socks made of cloth to show wind direction and speed. The socks fill with air and point in the direction the wind is blowing.

Today's weather forecasters measure wind speed with an instrument called an anemometer. Most anemometers have several cups that spin when the wind blows. The anemometer counts how often the cups spin around the center. This number tells forecasters how fast the wind is blowing.

You can tell how fast wind is blowing even without instruments. By observing the movements of flags, people, trees, and other objects outside, it is easy to see the difference between a strong wind and a light wind.

Anemometers are used to measure wind speed.

When we say a south wind is blowing, we mean the wind is blowing from the south.

MAKE A WEATHER VANE

1. Stick a pencil in a large lump of clay with the eraser end up. Be sure the pencil is steady.

2. Stick an arrowhead and tail made from cardboard in each end of a drinking straw.

3. Pin the straw onto the eraser.

4. Mark North, South, East, and West on the clay, and use a compass to position the wind vane on a wall or fence.

5. Watch the vane turn in the wind. In which direction is the wind blowing?

Soil Erosion

Although wind is made of air, it can be more powerful than rock.

Given enough time, wind can wear away earth and rock. This process is called **erosion**.

In dry areas, wind carries sand and dust. The force of the wind blasts rock and other objects with the tiny grains of sand. Over time, rocks can form odd shapes as softer rock is worn away, leaving the harder rock underneath.

Each year, tons of soil are carried to oceans or lakes by the wind. The United States loses more than one billion tons of soil a year from its farmlands due to erosion by wind. Asia loses about 25 billion tons. Losing good soil makes it more difficult to grow enough crops to feed people.

Sand and dust blown from one area can settle in other areas. Wind can blow unprotected soil hundreds of miles before dropping it. Desert lands in many parts of the world are increasing. Part of this increase is due to sand

Dust storms like this one remove valuable topsoil from farmland.

carried by wind. In some areas, the Sahara Desert is moving south at a rate of 328 feet (100 m) per year.

BYTE-SIZED FACT

Wind has buried the Great Sphinx up to its neck in sand several times in its history. The Great Sphinx stands about 66 feet (20 m) tall in the desert near Giza, Egypt. Workers removed sand from around the sculpture in 1818, 1886, 1926, and 1938.

What are air currents?

Imagine that Earth is a big, smooth ball of soil, with no water or mountains. Now imagine that it stops rotating, so it is standing still. If Earth were like this, the land at the equator would get the most heat, and air currents would always be the same. The heated air would rise and pull cooler air from both the north and south. When air rises, it expands because the pressure is lower at higher **altitudes**. Expanding air cools. The cooling air above ground would flow both north and south from the equator, then sink down, pushing the air below toward the equator. Air would form regular loops from the equator to the poles. Winds would always blow north and south from the poles to the equator.

Earth's rotation disturbs these ideal patterns. The air sinks to the surface before reaching the poles, causing the trade winds to blow. The same thing happens when cold air moves from the poles. More than one "loop" of air helps make the world's air currents. Lakes, oceans, prairies, and mountains also disturb the smooth flow of air.

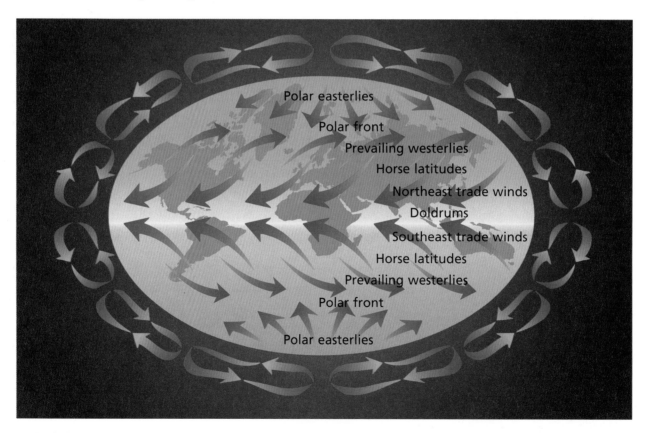

Polar easterlies
Polar front
Prevailing westerlies
Horse latitudes
Northeast trade winds
Doldrums
Southeast trade winds
Horse latitudes
Prevailing westerlies
Polar front
Polar easterlies

Winds blowing north and south do not move in straight lines because Earth's rotation moves them slightly. This is why some winds blow from the southeast and northeast instead of straight from the north and south.

Wind Power

Wind has been used as a source of power for hundreds of years. It was once used to grind grains into flour and to pump water.

Some of today's windmills produce electricity. As the wind blows, it turns the blades of a windmill. This movement operates machines that produce electricity.

Wind has also been used as a source of power for transportation. At one time, the only way to cross the Atlantic Ocean was by ships with sails. If the winds did not blow, sailors did not sail. Luckily, the main east to west winds are so regular that merchants could count on them to get their products delivered on time. Sailors called these winds the trade winds.

Today most people cross the oceans by airplane. Planes traveling from east to west, or west to east, can use a series of winds high in the atmosphere called the **jet stream**. Air in the jet stream can move at 224 miles per hour (360 kph). Pilots use the jet stream to shorten flights from North America to Europe by 1 hour.

In some places, hundreds of windmills are built on wind farms. Some wind farms can produce enough electricity to supply towns and cities.

BYTE-SIZED FACT

In some areas, winds follow a regular pattern. The direction the wind blows from most often is called the "prevailing wind." These winds can deform the growth of trees.

What turns wind into a twister?

Tornadoes can happen during severe thunderstorms. Only 1 in 1,000 thunderstorms produces a tornado. Winds in a tornado can reach 150 to 200 miles per hour (240 to 320 kph). Many tornadoes never touch the ground, but those that do suck up dirt, debris, and other objects. Tornadoes can even lift cars off the ground and completely destroy houses and other buildings. Roughly 1,000 tornadoes occur in North America every year.

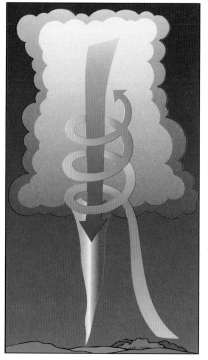

1. Wild winds form inside thunderclouds as warm air moves in below cool air that is moving in a different direction.

2. Winds higher up in the cloud blow faster and in a different direction than winds below. The air begins to spin. As the air spins faster and faster, it becomes a column.

3. The funnel of spinning air pushes down through the cloud toward the ground.

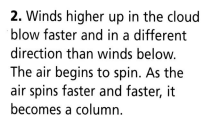

BYTE-SIZED FACT

The states of Kansas, Oklahoma, and Missouri are known as "Tornado Alley." These states have more tornadoes than anywhere else on Earth—more than 700 each year.

Storm Chaser

Most people try to stay as far away from tornadoes as possible. Yet some people go out of their way to get as close as possible to tornadoes.

These people, called "tornado hunters" or "storm chasers," are not always scientists, but they are well trained in tornado safety. They use video cameras and other instruments to gather information about tornadoes. The information is then given to scientists who study tornadoes.

Even tiny objects thrown by a tornado at 186 miles per hour (300 kph) can be deadly. For example, a piece of straw traveling at that speed can kill.

Storm chasers listen to current weather information for clues about where a tornado might happen next. While heading toward a potential tornado, they get information from weather stations by radio, telephone, and television. If a tornado appears, the storm chasers have only a few minutes to set up equipment that will help them observe the storm. Video cameras record the tornado. Tornado hunters may also carry a TOTO (Totable Tornado Observatory), or its newer version, called the Turtle, to measure the temperature, wind speed, and air pressure inside a tornado.

Anything directly in a tornado's path can be destroyed. Amazingly, objects just a few feet to its side can escape untouched.

What is El Niño?

Early Spanish sailors noticed periodic changes in water temperatures where they fished off the west coast of South America. They called the rise in temperature El Niño, meaning "Christ Child," because it always happened just after Christmas. The change happened about once every seven years.

Peru's cool coastal waters normally have some of the best fishing areas in the world. During El Niño, however, a change in wind patterns causes the water to warm. The ocean currents change, and the best fishing waters surface far from shore.

The shifting patterns of El Niño have many other effects. There are changes in temperature and wind patterns around the world. El Niño has been blamed for everything from **droughts** in Africa and Australia to floods in California. Some people believe it has even caused outbreaks of tropical diseases.

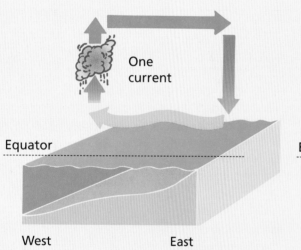

Normal conditions: When winds blow across the oceans, they produce systems of ocean currents. Air above the warm water north of Australia rises and then cools as it travels toward the west coast of South America, high above the Pacific Ocean. The cool air then drops down and travels back across the Pacific Ocean.

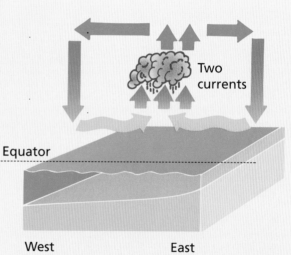

El Niño conditions: The warm spot moves from Australia to the middle of the Pacific, near Tahiti. Rising air circulates both east and west, making two loops. The waters off Peru become warmer, and the nutrient-rich waters surface farther from shore.

Wind Shears

Wind, fog, thunderstorms, blizzards, extremes of temperature, and air pressure—almost all weather conditions affect pilots and how safely they can fly their aircraft.

Airplanes that are taking off and landing are especially vulnerable to wind conditions. Sudden changes of wind speed or direction—known as wind shears—are the biggest threat. Wind shears are caused by fast-moving streams of air, called microbursts, that plunge directly downward to the

ground. When they hit the ground, microbursts spread out in all directions for up to 2.5 miles (4 km). Wind shears are violent, powerful, and unpredictable. Large or small, any airplane hitting a wind shear at 500 feet (150 m) or lower has little chance of recovery.

Wind shears were responsible for 626 deaths in the United States between 1964 and 1985. Radar instruments now help airlines find microbursts.

BYTE-SIZED FACT

Weather can create expenses for business and industry. For example:
- Each hour a train is delayed costs $2,000.
- Every airline flight that is canceled costs the airline $40,000.

- Each rig that is prevented from drilling for oil or natural gas costs the drilling company $250,000 per day.
- Each year, the vegetable processing industry (freezing and canning of foods) loses $42.5 million due to bad weather.

Water

"There's a 60 percent chance of showers today."

Without water, there would be no weather. Water vapor in the air interacts with heat from the Sun to create weather patterns on Earth. Weather only happens in the region of the atmosphere that is about 6 miles (10 km) above the Earth. This region is called the troposphere. Only the troposphere contains water vapor that has been evaporated from Earth's surface.

How can there be water in the air?

Water vapor is invisible, but even on a bright, clear, cloudless day, there is water vapor in the air. When the sun shines on oceans, lakes, rivers, and ponds, it always causes some water to evaporate. Evaporation means that water turns from a liquid that you can see into a gas that you cannot see.

There is a limit to the amount of water vapor that the air can hold. If you try to add more, some of the vapor will **condense**, or turn into liquid water. The temperature of the air determines how much water it can hold. Warm air holds much more water than cold. For example, air at 86°F (30°C) can hold more than six times as much water vapor as air at 32°F (0°C).

Dew forms when surfaces near the ground become cool enough for water vapor in the air to condense. When warm, moist air reaches the temperature at which it cannot hold water in a gas form, it has reached the **dewpoint**. Beads of water then appear on surfaces.

BYTE-SIZED FACT
The air in your lungs holds as much water vapor as possible. The water vapor is the same temperature as your body: 98.6°F (37°C). When you breathe out in the winter, the warm air from your body combines with cold air that cannot hold as much water vapor. When you "see" your breath, some of the water vapor has condensed into tiny droplets of water.

What are clouds, and how do they form?

Clouds are made of tiny droplets of water or ice crystals in the air. When warm, moist air meets cooler air, some warm air cools and cannot hold all of its water vapor. Some of the extra water changes into a liquid or even freezes. This forms clouds.

Clouds come in a variety of sizes and shapes. Most clouds belong to one of three basic categories: cumulus, stratus, or cirrus. You may also see the word "nimbus" added to a cloud name. For example, a cumulonimbus cloud is a rain cloud.

Cumulus clouds are puffy with flat bottoms. These clouds can be as high as 14,000 feet (4,267 m) in the air. Cumulus clouds often form on warm summer days and then disappear at night.

Stratus clouds form quite low and often cover the sky like a gray sheet. The clouds barely move, and the air under them is very still. These conditions can make the sky look dull and heavy.

Cirrus clouds are made of ice crystals. They form very high in the sky, usually above 25,000 feet (7,620 m). Cirrus clouds have a wispy, feathery appearance. The winds blow cirrus clouds into fine strands that are sometimes called "mares' tails."

BYTE-SIZED FACT

Airplanes make cirrus clouds when water vapor from their engines forms ice crystals. The clouds look like long streaks high in the sky.

Fog & Smog

Fog and mist form when warm, moist air passes over a cold surface, such as the ground at night.

The air is cooled below the dewpoint, and a cloud forms. Fog is a cloud that forms close to the ground.

Smog is a kind of fog that is mixed with chemicals. The word smog is a combination of the words "smoke" and "fog." In 1905, when the word was first used, smog was made of smoke and fog.

Today smog is a combination of fog and chemicals given off by factories and cars. The chemicals and water vapor are "cooked" by the Sun to form smog. Cities with more fog also tend to have more smog. From a distance, smog looks like a yellowish blanket lying low over the city.

People who breathe in a great deal of smog can develop **bronchitis**. Smog can also wear away buildings.

If you can see fewer than 0.5 miles (0.8 km) through mist on the ground, it is called fog. If you can see between 0.5 miles and 1 mile (0.8 and 1.6 km), it is considered a mist.

BYTE-SIZED FACT

A "killer smog" hit London, England, in 1952. After 5 days, 4,000 people had died. In the 1950s London made laws to restrict the kinds and amounts of pollution allowed into the air.

Why does rain fall?

A cloud droplet has a million times less water than a typical raindrop. Cloud droplets are very light and tiny. Stormy air in the sky tosses small droplets around so much that they usually cannot fall to the ground. They will not fall until they collide with each other and join together to make larger, heavier droplets.

If the air is very still, smaller drops may fall to the ground as the form of rain we call drizzle. Larger raindrops usually start as ice crystals near the center of cumulus clouds. The ice crystals collect water from droplets in the clouds. The crystals grow larger and larger until they are heavy enough to fall through the **turbulent** air. While passing through warm air close to Earth, the crystals melt and turn into raindrops. If the air temperature remains cold, the ice crystals do not melt and fall as snow.

Drops of water more than 0.02 inches (0.05 cm) in size are rain. Drops smaller than this are called drizzle.

During a severe storm, air currents may push upward so violently that they carry growing ice crystals and pellets high into the clouds. Water continues to condense on the crystals until they grow very large. When the ice balls finally fall through the warmer air below, they are too big to completely melt. They fall as hailstones.

Snowflakes form from ice crystals. If the air warms up as they fall, snowflakes become raindrops.

Raindrops are shaped like disks, not teardrops. Raindrops are round when they leave the clouds, but the wind resistance on the way to Earth flattens them slightly.

BYTE-SIZED FACT

How do we measure rain and humidity?

Rain gauges are instruments that collect and measure water that falls during a 24-hour period. A rain gauge is a hollow cylinder that is usually about 20 inches (50 cm) high. It is placed high enough off the ground so that water will not splash into it. Rainwater runs down a funnel at the top of the cylinder and is collected and measured in the base.

Humidity is measured with a hygrometer. A simple hygrometer uses two thermometers. One of the thermometers is surrounded by a wet cloth. If the air is wet, or humid, the two thermometers will have similar temperatures.

If the air is dry, the moisture in the wet cloth will evaporate, cooling down that thermometer. The difference between the two temperature readings gives the level of humidity in the air. Understanding humidity can help scientists predict rain, snow, fog, clouds, and icy conditions.

This rain gauge has collected 2.4 inches (6 cm) of water.

BYTE-SIZED FACT

Your hair is longer in humid weather than in dry weather. As hair becomes full of water vapor, its length increases by about 3 percent. The first hygrometers used hair to measure humidity. First a long piece of hair was boiled in chemicals to remove any natural oils. Then the hair was tied to a needle. The needle moved as the hair got longer or shorter. Longer hair meant more humidity, and a likely chance of rain.

The hygrometer in this kit (on the right, next to the two thermometers) is used to measure humidity in the air.

Making Rain

For as long as we have tried to understand and predict the weather, we have tried to control it. So far, however, our success has been limited.

A partial success is the discovery of cloud seeding. An airplane drops chemical particles, sprayed water, or salt on top of a cloud. The material acts like a seed onto which water droplets can attach. The water droplets become heavy enough to fall to Earth as rain.

This type of rainmaking has helped many areas that do not get enough rain. This system has also been used to help prevent dangerous storms, such as hurricanes. By forcing storm clouds to release some of their water, a serious storm can be turned into smaller rain clouds.

Special equipment attached to the wing of an airplane drops materials on top of clouds to produce rain.

BYTE-SIZED FACT

In Chile, scientists are trying to catch clouds in nets that are about 39 feet (12 m) long and 13 feet (4 m) wide. When fogs blow into the nets, the mesh strains raindrops of water. The scientists have had some success with this method—it sometimes yields 2,500 gallons (9,500 l) of water per day.

How is a thunderstorm different from an ordinary rainstorm?

A thunderstorm has very violent winds with thunder and lightning. Clouds may rise as high as 14 miles (22 km). The energy of a thunderstorm is much greater than the energy of an atomic bomb!

Thunderstorms often occur after a long period of hot weather. This is because the ground becomes very warm from the heat of the Sun.

A thunderstorm begins when drafts of warm air move upward, creating a large cumulus cloud. When the cloud is high enough for the rain to begin, the thunderstorm is mature. As rain falls through the cloud, it cools the air, causing downdrafts. The air in the cloud becomes very turbulent. Finally, the rain cools all of the air in the cloud until there are no more updrafts. The rain stops, and winds scatter the cloud.

BYTE-SIZED FACT

You can tell whether a thunderstorm or just rain is coming by looking at clouds in the distance. Tall clouds mean a thunderstorm is on the way. Thinner clouds will bring a slower and steadier rain.

What causes lightning and thunder?

Ice particles and raindrops in clouds are made of molecules. Collisions between ice particles and raindrops break negatively charged particles, called electrons, off their molecules. When a particle loses electrons, it becomes positively charged. These positively charged particles cause nearby particles to become negatively charged. Positive charges collect in the top part of the thundercloud, while clusters of negative charges collect at the bottom. The ground becomes charged as well. Opposite charges attract each other with such a strong force that the charges leap from cloud to cloud or between clouds and the ground. This giant electric spark is lightning.

When lightning strikes, it instantly heats the air. The quick expansion of the warm air starts a shock wave that you hear as thunder. Lightning and thunder happen at the same time, but thunder is heard later because light travels faster than sound.

When you see a zigzag pattern in lightning, it is called forked lightning. If the lightning is reflected over a wide area, it is called sheet lightning.

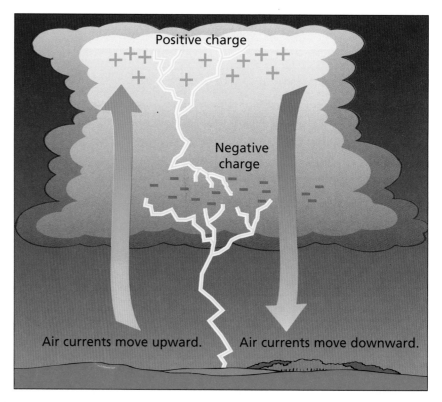

Positive charge

Negative charge

Air currents move upward.   Air currents move downward.

POINTS OF VIEW

Water, Water ... Everywhere?

Earth is often called the "water planet," since about 70 percent of its surface is covered with water. However, less than 3 percent of all the world's water is fresh, drinkable, and accessible!

With such a limited supply of **freshwater**, a weather disaster such as a drought can cause serious problems. For example, the Mississippi River is the United States' most important inland route for transporting products by boat. Inland barges and tugboats can carry their cargoes more than 1,800 miles (2,900 km) south, to the Gulf of Mexico. In 1988 a severe drought dried up so much of the river that boat traffic had to stop.

In desperation, the state of Illinois decided it could increase the amount of water in the river by draining water from Lake Michigan and Lake Huron, two of the five Great Lakes. These lakes contain almost one-fifth of the entire world's freshwater. Other states that border Lake Michigan and Lake Huron objected to the plan. So did the government of Canada. In the end, the drainage plan was abandoned.

"The Mississippi River is essential for shipping the products from businesses in my state. The Great Lakes have plenty of water—why shouldn't we put the water to use?" **Politician in Illinois**

"It is unfortunate that the Mississippi River is drying up, but draining the lakes won't solve the problem. Our state uses the lakes for transportation." **Politician in Minnesota**

"I can't wait anymore. If I can't get the goods I need from Illinois, I'm going to have to find other suppliers in different parts of the country." **Manager of a plant waiting for goods to be delivered from upriver**

"The Great Lakes are a shared resource. No single country or state has the right to alter them for its own use." **Prime Minister of Canada**

What other points of view might there be in this conflict?
What is your point of view?
How is it similar to or different from the other points of view?

What causes a hurricane?

A hurricane happens when air currents near the equator begin to circulate, and several thunderstorms are pulled together. Updrafts of warm, moist air form storm clouds, and the rain begins. The condensation of the water releases energy to strengthen the updrafts. At the top, the air moves out and begins to drop. Near the surface of the ocean, the air is drawn back toward the center. The air picks up more moisture from the warm ocean and creates more updrafts. The cycle continues, and the storm grows.

As long as the hurricane is over water, it can maintain or increase its strength. When it moves onto land, it causes enormous damage to lives and to property in its path. But when it runs out of water, the hurricane loses energy and dies out.

Hurricanes need an unlimited supply of water and heat. Only tropical oceans have these two things. Hurricane Georges caused severe damage in the Caribbean and the southern United States when it struck in September 1998.

How are hurricanes measured?

Not all hurricanes are the same. The Saffir/Simpson Hurricane Scale is used by forecasters working for the United States government to issue hurricane warnings. This scale estimates not only wind speed, but also storm surges—how far tides are being blown onto the land. There are five categories on the scale.

	Wind speed	Storm surge	Damage
1	74–95 mph 120–152 kph	4–5 feet 1–1.5 m	trees lose twigs and leaves; mobile homes damaged
2	96–110 mph 154–176 kph	6–8 feet 2–2.4 m	small trees blown down; mobile homes severely damaged
3	111–130 mph 180–210 kph	9–12 feet 2.7–3.6 m	large trees blown down; mobile homes destroyed; some buildings damaged
4	131–155 mph 210–250 kph	13–18 feet 4–5.5 m	windows, roofs, and doors of buildings damaged; flooding to 6 miles (10 km) inland
5	> 155 mph > 250 kph	> 18 feet > 5.5 m	all buildings damaged; smaller buildings destroyed

Satellites

Satellites take pictures and measure the temperature of clouds, the ground, and water. They also allow scientists to send weather information quickly to other weather stations around the world.

Weather satellites take three different types of photographs of Earth: visible, infrared, and water vapor. Visible images are just like the photographs you take with a camera, but from high up in space. They allow us to see both cloud formations and snow accumulations.

Infrared images are photographs of temperature. Warm temperatures show up as dark areas, while cold areas look lighter gray. Very cold areas, such as a high cloud or the top of a tall thunderstorm cloud, are white. Satellites can also take enhanced infrared images that show clouds in color. These help scientists spot serious thunderstorm clouds.

Water vapor images take pictures of the water droplets in the sky. Dark areas have very little water in the air, while gray areas have a lot of water. These images allow scientists to track the movements of the jet stream.

Infrared shots of Earth help meteorologists track the formation of thunderstorms that might lead to hurricanes.

A satellite photo of Hurricane Fran warned meteorologists of the storm's approach.

Are you prepared for a weather emergency? In 1997 the American Red Cross and The Weather Channel conducted a survey of 2,039 Americans, aged 18 or older. They were asked a variety of questions to find out how prepared people are in case of a weather-related disaster such as a flood, blizzard, hurricane, or tornado.

What are your answers?

1. Do you believe that a weather-related disaster like a flood or hurricane could happen where you live?
2. Would you and your family be prepared if a weather emergency happened right now?
3. Have you and your family prepared an emergency supply kit to get you through a weather disaster?
4. Have you and your family ever practiced what to do in case of an emergency?
5. Would you know what to do and where to go if you were told to evacuate your home?
6. Do you or any family members have any first aid training?

Piles of sandbags block the rising water from a flood.

Survey Results

Nearly every day, reporters and news broadcasters cover stories about weather-related disasters such as droughts, heat waves, cold snaps, tornadoes, and floods.

And yet, more than half of the people surveyed believed that a weather-related disaster was unlikely to happen where they live. Only 1 in 6 people believed such an event was very likely to happen. And only 1 in 7 people said they would be completely prepared if a weather emergency were to happen right now.

Here is your challenge:

What would you keep in your emergency supply kit?

Make a list of all the items you would keep in an emergency supply kit. Use the questions below to guide your choices.

1. Will you need water? How much?
2. What about food? How much, and what kinds?
3. What first aid supplies do you need?
4. What if there is no electricity available?
5. What kinds of clothing will keep you warm (or cool)?
6. What will you sleep on?
7. How will you see in the dark?
8. What if it rains or snows?
9. What if someone gets sick?
10. If you have younger sisters or brothers, what do they need?
11. If you have pets, what do they need?
12. How will you keep yourself entertained if you are stuck in a shelter for days or weeks?
13. Is there anything else to consider?

Fast Facts

1. The Atacama Desert in Chile receives less than 1/250 of an inch (1/10 of a mm) of rain each year.

2. Nearly 1,000 square miles (2,590 sq km) of land in China are turning to desert each year. Drought is one of the causes of this disaster, along with erosion and overgrazing by livestock.

3. In the eastern Sahara Desert, the Sun shines for 97 percent of possible daylight hours.

4. The highest recorded temperature in the United States was 134°F (56.7°C) in Death Valley, California, on July 10, 1913.

5. The lowest recorded temperature in the United States was –79.8°F (–62.1°C) in Prospect Creek Camp, Alaska, on January 23, 1971.

6. Antarctica is getting warmer. During the last 50 years, the average temperature has increased by 4.5°F (2.5°C).

7. Overexposure to the Sun is a major cause of skin cancer.

8. Hurricanes have a center known as the "eye." The storm is shaped like a doughnut with a calm hole. During a hurricane, the eye can become full of birds flying to keep out of the storm.

9. The windiest place in the world is Commonwealth Bay, on the coast of Antarctica. Winds there can reach speeds of 200 miles per hour (320 kph).

10. The United States has more tornadoes than any other country in the world.

11. Windchill occurs when the wind blows away the thin layer of warm air that normally surrounds your body.

12. In the Northern Hemisphere, tornadoes spin in a counter-clockwise direction. In the Southern Hemisphere, they spin in a clockwise direction.

13. If there were no wind, there would be little or no day-to-day change in our weather.

14. The world record for the highest wind speed is 231 miles per hour (370 kph). It was recorded at the summit of Mount Washington in New Hampshire.

15. The largest snowflake ever recorded measured 15 inches (38 cm) across.

16. Hail can hit the ground at 80 miles per hour (130 kph).

17. In the United States, an average of 80 people die every year as a result of being struck by lightning. You have a better chance of being struck by lightning twice in your life than of winning a big lottery.

18. The largest hailstone ever recorded was 17 inches (42.5 cm) in diameter.

19. The Yellow River, or Hwang Ho, in China has been nicknamed "China's Sorrow" because it has killed more people by floods than any other river in the world.

20. For a hurricane to develop, the ocean surface must have a temperature of at least 78°F (25.5°C).

Young Scientists@Work

Test your weather knowledge with these questions and activities. You can probably answer the questions using only this book, your own experiences, and your common sense.

FACT:

Coastal areas have warmer summers and milder winters than inland areas.

TEST:

You can do an experiment to show how water affects temperature. Place an empty glass and a glass full of water in the refrigerator.

Wait 15 minutes. Then take the glasses out of the refrigerator.

PREDICT:

Which glass will feel warmer? Look back to page 10 if you need a clue.

FACT:

One of the best ways to measure wind speed is by observing the effects of wind. Admiral Francis Beaufort designed a wind scale in the 1800s to help sailors judge wind speed. Today's Beaufort scale has been adapted for use on land.

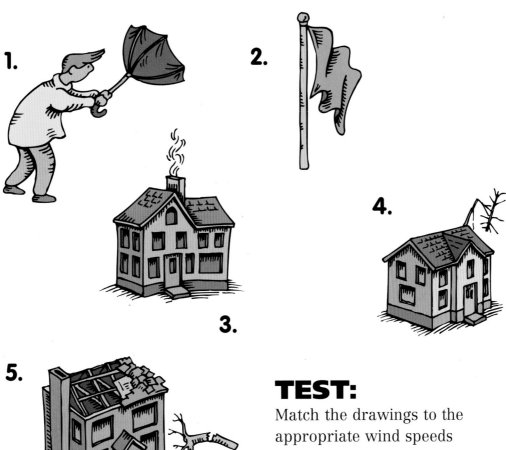

1.

2.

3.

4.

5.

TEST:

Match the drawings to the appropriate wind speeds from the Beaufort scale.

a. less than 1 mph (1.6 kph)
b. 8–12 mph (13–19 kph)
c. 25–31 mph (40–50 kph)
d. 47–54 mph (76–87 kph)
e. more than 75 mph (121 kph)

Answers:
1-c, 2-b, 3-a, 4-d, 5-e.

Research on Your Own

There are many places to find out more about weather. Your local library, weather station, and the Internet will all have excellent resources and information for you.

Here are some awesome weather resources for you to try:

Great Books

Branley, Franklin. *Flash, Crash, Rumble, and Roll.* New York: Thomas Y. Crowell, 1985.

Cosgrove, Brian. *Eyewitness Books, Weather.* New York: Alfred A. Knopf Inc., 1991.

Ganeri, Anita. *The Usborne Book of Weather Facts.* IEDC Publishing, 1992.

Mandel, Muriel. *Simple Weather Experiments with Everyday Materials.* Sterling Publishing Co., 1990.

Great Websites

Amazing Weather Records
www.universe.digex.net/~wfci/infowrec.html

Dan's Wild Weather Page
www.whnt19.com/kidwx

Skywatchers Observations
www.weatheroffice.com

World Meteorological Organization
www.wmo.ch/web-en/wmofact.html

Glossary

acid rain: Rain that contains pollutants mixed with water vapor.

altitude: Distance above sea level

atmosphere: The layers of gases that surround Earth. The layers closest to Earth contain more air than the layers farther away.

axis: The imaginary line on which Earth rotates

bronchitis: A sickness in the lungs

chlorofluorocarbon (CFC): A type of chemical found in refrigerators and sprays that damages the ozone layer

condense: When gas or vapor changes into liquid

dewpoint: The temperature at which water vapor begins to condense

drought: A long period of dry weather

ecosystem: A natural community of living things in their environment

equator: An imaginary line around Earth halfway between the poles

erosion: The wearing away of Earth's surface due to wind and water

evaporate: When liquid water changes into vapor

freshwater: Water that is not salty

hemisphere: Half of Earth divided at the equator

humidity: The amount of water vapor in the air

infrared: Invisible rays from the Sun that we feel as heat

jet stream: Strong westerly winds concentrated in a narrow stream

melanin: A substance in the skin that causes it to become brown

mercury: A heavy, liquid, metallic element

meteorology: The study of what happens in the atmosphere, especially as it concerns predicting weather

molecules: The smallest particles of a substance, composed of one or more atoms

orbit: The curved path of a planet, moon, or satellite around another body

solar panels: Devices that produce electricity when sunlight hits them

tropical: Warm regions near the equator that get a great deal of sunshine all year-round

turbulent: A disturbance in a flow of air or water

Index